101 Facts About

101 FACTS ABOUT

LAKES

Julia Barnes

Gareth Stevens Publishing
A WORLD ALMANAC EDUCATION GROUP COMPANY

Please visit our web site at: www.garethstevens.com
For a free color catalog describing Gareth Stevens Publishing's
list of high-quality books and multimedia programs,
call 1-800-542-2595 (USA) or 1-800-387-3178 (Canada).
Gareth Stevens Publishing's fax: (414) 332-3567.

Library of Congress Cataloging-in-Publication Data

Barnes, Julia, 1955-
    101 facts about lakes / by Julia Barnes. — North American ed.
      p. cm. — (101 facts about our world)
    Summary: Describes the characteristics, formation, plant and animal life,
and preservation of lakes.
    Includes bibliographical references and index.
    ISBN 0-8368-3707-X (lib. bdg.)
    1. Lake ecology—Juvenile literature. 2. Lakes—Juvenile literature. [1. Lakes.
2. Lake ecology. 3. Ecology.] I. Title: One hundred one facts about lakes.
II. Title: One hundred and one facts about lakes. III. Title: Lakes. IV. Title.
QH541.5.L3B37   2003
551.48'2—dc21   2003050484

This North American edition first published in 2004 by
Gareth Stevens Publishing
A World Almanac Education Group Company
330 West Olive Street, Suite 100
Milwaukee, WI 53212 USA

This U.S. edition copyright © 2004 by Gareth Stevens, Inc. Original edition © 2003 by First
Stone Publishing. First published by First Stone Publishing, 4/5 The Marina, Harbour
Road, Lydney, Gloucestershire, GL15 5ET, United Kingdom. Additional end matter © 2004
by Gareth Stevens, Inc.

First Stone Series Editor: Claire Horton-Bussey
First Stone Designer: Rob Benson
Geographical consultant: Miles Ellison
Gareth Stevens Editors: Catherine Gardner and JoAnn Early Macken

Photographs © Oxford Scientific Films Ltd

Printed in Hong Kong through Printworks Int. Ltd

1 2 3 4 5 6 7 8 9 07 06 05 04 03

On the surface, it looks as if little happens in a lake. Unlike rivers, lakes do not have fast-flowing water, crashing waterfalls, or rushing rapids. A lake's secrets lie in its stillness.

A lake is surrounded by land, which protects its water from major disturbances. The calm water offers an ideal home for plants and fish, which attract fish-eating birds as well as animals that come to drink at the shoreline. Lakes are valuable to us for fishing and as a source of freshwater.

Some people do not take good care of lakes. If we do not protect lakes, their freshwater and all the living things that need it will be in danger.

MAJOR LAKES OF THE WORLD

Great Bear Lake

Great Slave Lake

Lake Athabasca

NORTH AMERICA

Lake Superior

Lake Huron

North Pacific Ocean

North Atlantic Ocean

Lake Winnipeg

Crater Lake

Beaver Lake

Great Salt Lake

Lake Ontario

Lake Erie

Lake Michigan

SOUTH AMERICA

South Pacific Ocean

South Atlantic Ocean

Lake Titicaca

Key

Division between North and South America

Division between Asia and Africa

Division between Europe and Asia

Division between Asia and Oceania

AUSTRALIAN LAKES
1. Lake Mackay
2. Lake Disappointment
3. Lake Carnegie
4. Lake Barlee
5. Lake Moore
6. Lake Cowan
7. Lake Amadeus
8. Lake Gairdner
9. Lake Torrens
10. Lake Eyre

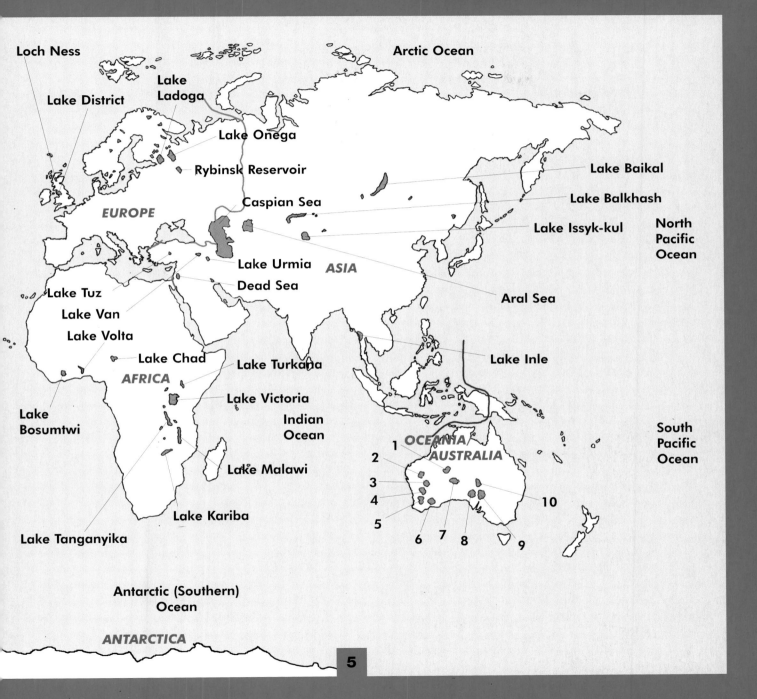

Loch Ness

Lake District

Lake Ladoga

Lake Onega

Rybinsk Reservoir

Caspian Sea

EUROPE

Lake Tuz

Lake Van

Lake Volta

Lake Chad

AFRICA

Lake Bosumtwi

Lake Urmia

Dead Sea

ASIA

Lake Turkana

Lake Victoria

Indian Ocean

Lake Malawi

Lake Kariba

Lake Tanganyika

Arctic Ocean

Lake Baikal

Lake Balkhash

Lake Issyk-kul

North Pacific Ocean

Aral Sea

Lake Inle

OCEANIA

AUSTRALIA

1
2
3
4
5
6
7
8
9
10

South Pacific Ocean

Antarctic (Southern) Ocean

ANTARCTICA

1 All lakes are areas of water surrounded by land. Not all lakes are the same, however. They have different weather, different wildlife, and even different kinds of water.

2 Some lakes dry up in the hottest months, and others freeze over in winter.

3 Lakes may contain salt water, which is the kind of water that is also found in oceans. Lakes that do not have salt water are called **freshwater** lakes.

4 Lakes may be quite small or very big. Tiny lakes are usually called ponds. Some of the largest lakes are known as seas.

5 The Caspian Sea, between Europe and Asia, is the largest lake on Earth. It covers 143,244 square miles (371,002 square kilometers).

6 The deepest lake is Lake Baikal in Russia. It is about 1 mile (1.6 km) deep in some spots, and it contains one-fifth of Earth's unfrozen freshwater.

7 Lakes do not stay the same. The forces of nature can create new lakes and make existing lakes bigger or smaller.

8 As lakes age, they can shrink. Rivers (above) bring in gravel, mud, and sand, called **sediment**.

9 In a lake that has a lot of sediment, plants take root. Plants can turn a lake into a **marshland** or even a grassy **meadow**.

10 Some lakes have short lives. When the main flow of a river cuts off a meander, or big bend, it forms a small lake called an **oxbow lake** (above).

11 Unless an oxbow lake is fed by a new supply of water, it disappears. The water **evaporates** into the air.

12 Most big lakes last for thousands of years – and a few have been great survivors.

13 Lake Baikal is the oldest freshwater lake on Earth. It began to take shape about 25 million years ago. Lake Baikal (right) holds more water than any other freshwater lake.

14 Lake Baikal began when movements of Earth's crust, or outer layer, produced a huge crack in the ground.

15 Rainwater and river water collected in the deep crack, and Lake Baikal took shape.

16 Lake Baikal receives water from more than 300 rivers. Along with the water, the lake receives all the sediment that flows in with the rivers.

17 Sediment falls to the bottom of a lake. The sediment layer in Lake Baikal is believed to be more than 4 miles (6 km) thick.

18 Like any lake, even the gigantic Lake Baikal could slowly fill with sediment. Millions of years from now, a meadow may take the place of the lake.

19 In places where Earth's crust cracks, land may fall between the cracks to form a long, thin valley, called a rift valley.

20 Water can collect in a rift valley to form long, thin lakes. The Great Rift Valley in Africa includes many of these narrow lakes, such as Lake Malawi and Lake Tanganyika (left).

21 At the northern end of the Great Rift Valley, between Israel and Jordan, is the Dead Sea. The Dead Sea is really a saltwater lake.

22 The Dead Sea marks the lowest point on Earth's surface. This lake is 1,312 feet (400 meters) below sea level.

23 The highest lake on Earth is Lake Titicaca in South America. This lake is 12,500 feet (3,800 m) above sea level.

24 Some of the biggest lakes were created during the last **Ice Age**, which began about 70,000 years ago.

25 Glaciers (above), which are like huge rivers of ice, formed on Earth and inched their way slowly across the ice-covered land.

26 Glaciers scooped out big holes in the ground. When the ice melted at the end of the Ice Age, these holes filled with water.

28 The glaciers carried enormous boulders, and when the ice eventually melted, these huge rocks were left on the land.

29 Sometimes, the boulders blocked the ends of valleys. Rain and river water built up behind the boulders to form lakes, like those of the Lake District in northern England.

27 The Great Lakes of North America lie in a **basin** that was carved by glaciers and by the huge weight of snow that covered the continent.

30 Deep under Earth's surface is a layer of red-hot liquid rock. When a **volcano** erupts (left), this liquid rock blasts out of the ground, creating a crater, or hole, in the ground.

31 When a volcano no longer erupts, its crater can collect water and become a lake (below).

32 Crater Lake is in the crater of Mount Mazama, which is part of the Cascade Mountains in the United States.

33 Shaped like a circle, Crater Lake measures almost 6 miles (10 km)

across. It is the deepest lake in the United States.

34 The strangest type of lake had its start in outer space.

35 Lake Bosumtwi, in Africa, formed when a **meteorite** hit Earth and created a crater that filled with water.

across a river. River water builds up behind the dam in a quiet pool, where beavers build their **lodges**.

36 Some lakes start under the ground, where water **dissolves** rock. The upper surface of the land collapses, creating a **sinkhole** filled with water.

37 Beavers can make lakes, too. They start by building a dam (above)

38 Beaver Lake, which is in Yellowstone National Park in the United States, is an example of an artificial lake that is entirely the work of beavers.

39 Some spectacular lakes have been created by people.

40 People have built big dams that hold back river water. The water floods the land behind the dam, forming a lake called a **reservoir** (right).

41 Water in a reservoir may supply drinking water in a city or operate hydroelectric power stations.

42 Lake Volta in Ghana, one of the world's largest reservoirs, covers an area of 3,275 square miles (8,482 square km).

43 Usually, rivers or streams flow into and out of lakes. This flow keeps the lake water fresh.

44 Water flowing in from rivers and streams refills a lake. Water flowing out of a lake carries away salt, other minerals, and chemicals.

45 Lakes can lose more water than they gain from rivers or rain.

46 Evaporation is one way lakes can lose water. Heat changes water to a gas but leaves behind salt and other minerals.

47 As water in a lake evaporates, more and more minerals build up in the remaining water.

48 Water evaporates from the Dead Sea (below) faster than it flows in. The Dead Sea is nine times more salty than an ocean.

49 The Dead Sea is a great place for a swim. People float more easily in salt water than they do in freshwater.

50 Most living things cannot survive in the Dead Sea.

51 In hot and dry conditions, water evaporates quickly. The Great Salt Lake in Utah, in the United States, shrinks during the years of unusually hot weather.

52 In Antarctica, the cold weather affects the lakes. Many feet (meters) of ice may cover the surface of some lakes all year long.

53 The Onyx River flows into Lake Vanda in Antarctica for just a few weeks each summer.

54 Lake Vanda has a permanent covering of ice that is 13 feet (4 m) thick. Sunlight shines through

56 Freshwater lakes that are not frozen all year offer living conditions that are different from any other place on Earth (left). They do not have **currents** like rivers or oceans.

the clear ice, warming the temperature at the bottom of the lake to 77° Fahrenheit (25° Celsius).

55 In the sediment of Antarctica's lakes, scientists have found kinds of **algae** that could be like the first forms of life on Earth.

57 Water lilies and other plants (below) that float on the surface of a lake provide shelter to many different animals.

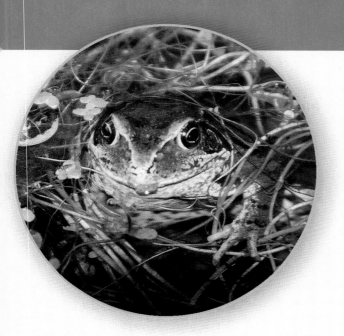

unique conditions that exist in a freshwater lake.

60 Usually, warm water flows through a lake, and colder water stays at the bottom.

58 A lake is like a miniature world, cut off from the land, yet with its own special community of plants and animals (above).

59 An amazing variety of fish, birds, and other animals have adapted, or learned to survive, in the

19

61 The water toward the bottom of a lake is cold and dark. Few plants and animals can live there.

62 Legends have grown up about monsters that lurk in the bottom of deep lakes. For example, some people say a giant sea monster lives in Loch Ness, Scotland.

63 Although scientists have searched for the Loch Ness monster, the legend remains a mystery.

64 In warm, shallow water, many kinds of plants and fish, such as the rudd (left), live together. The living things in a lake depend on each other for their survival.

65 Lake Baikal offers a home to more than 1,200 different **species** of animals and hundreds of different plants. Many of them live only in this lake.

66 One resident of Lake Baikal is the Baikal seal (right). One of the few seals that lives in freshwater, it is related to seals that live in the Arctic Ocean.

67 Scientists think the ancestors of Baikal seals traveled across the icy land during the Ice Age in search of food and adapted to the freshwater they found at Lake Baikal.

68 Another unusual animal in Lake Baikal is the golomyanka.

Unlike many kinds of fish, the golomyanka gives birth to live young.

69 Lake Tanganyika, in Africa, may be twenty million years old. It is home to many types of

fish, shrimps, and mussels that do not live anywhere else in the world.

70 About 130 species of cichlids and 50 other kinds of fish can be found only in the water of the ancient Lake Tanganyika.

71 Each species of cichlid (above) has a slightly different shape or color. Cichlids live in many different lakes and have different ways of breeding. Some kinds of cichlids are **mouth-brooders** (below).

72 In mouth-brooding cichlids, the eggs develop for many days and hatch while the mother holds them gently in her mouth.

73 Young cichlids stay in their mother's mouth for a week, protected from dangers in the lake.

74 For little fish, lakes are dangerous. In Lake Victoria in Africa, Nile perch can grow larger than a person. They have eaten some cichlids into extinction.

75 Where fish live, people who fish are usually not far away. In some lakeside communities, the people are as much at home on the water as they are on land.

76 The leg rowers of Lake Inle (right) in Myanmar have developed their own special boating skills. They guide their oars with one hand and one leg.

77 Many kinds of birds live on a diet of fish and must make their homes close to lakes.

23

78 Herons, storks, and egrets, which are long-legged wading birds, wait patiently in the shallows, ready to catch a fish if it rises to the surface.

79 Flamingos (below) live close to lakes, where they find their favorite foods: algae, shrimps, and insect larvae.

80 Using their long beaks, they strain the water to separate mud and sand from their food.

81 Pelicans (above) wade in the water, chasing fish to shallow spots. They open their beaks and scoop fish into their throat pouches. A pelican's pouch can hold about 2 gallons (7.5 liters) of water.

82 Ospreys (right) are fish-eating birds that fly high in the sky looking for fish in the water below.

83 When fish rise to the surface of the water, ospreys dive and catch them in their talons, or claws.

84 At the lake's edges, rushes, reeds, irises, and marsh marigolds grow in the deep soil.

85 Plants at the edge of a lake are visited by butterflies and many other insects. The dragonfly, which

hunts insects for food, hovers over the surface of the water.

86 On the lake's calm surface, water lilies and similar plants thrive.

87 Water lilies grow in all sizes and many climates. The biggest water lily grows in South America. It has huge matlike leaves.

88 Tropical birds called jacanas (below) can walk across the surface of a lake by stepping from one **lilypad** to the next.

89 Jacanas, nicknamed lily-trotters, stand on long, thin toes, which help spread out their weight and prevent them from sinking.

90 Otters (above) are super swimmers. They have webbed feet, and they can close off their ears and nostrils, allowing them to stay underwater for four to five minutes.

26

91 Lakes are not only important to the plants and animals that live in them. Large lakes can affect the climate of the land around them and provide drinking water for animals.

92 Large lakes in Africa, such as Lakes Tanganyika, Victoria, and Malawi, attract rhinoceroses, antelopes, zebras, giraffes (right), and big cats from dry grasslands to the refreshing water.

93 Hippopotamuses spend their days in the water of a lake or river. They leave the water at night to graze on grass.

94 The survival of animals, plants, and millions of people all around the world depends on having supplies of clean water.

95 Over the years, people have become careless about keeping lake water fresh and available.

96 Cities and factories sometimes dump waste into rivers, and the polluted water flows into lakes. Gas-powered boats also leave pollution.

97 Pollution upsets the delicate balance of life in lakes. When the water becomes too dirty, animals and plants start to die out.

98 People also **divert** rivers so the water flows to the crops in fields. Changing a river's path can leave a lake without a water supply and cause the lake to dry up (above).

99 The rivers that feed the Aral Sea in Asia were diverted, and the lake shrunk by half its size.

100 When we try to change nature without understanding all the ways that life-forms are connected, we risk harming the whole planet in ways that cannot be easily fixed.

101 Many plants and animals depend on lakes for their survival. In all their stages, lakes offer homes to a wide variety of wildlife. We must work hard to take care of them.

🌳 Glossary

algae: small plants without roots or stems that grow in water.

basin: an area of land that is lower than the surrounding land.

currents: movements of water in oceans or rivers.

dissolves: breaks down a solid material in a liquid.

divert: to turn aside.

evaporates: changes from water to vapor.

freshwater: water without a lot of salt or other minerals.

Ice Age: a period when much of Earth was covered by glaciers.

lilypad: floating leaf of a water lily.

lodges: the homes beavers build.

marshland: a low-lying area of wet ground.

meadow: low-lying grassland.

meteorite: a lump of solid rock from outer space.

mouth-brooder: a fish that allows its eggs to hatch in its mouth.

oxbow lake: a lake formed when a river bend is cut off from the main flow of the river.

reservoir: an artificial lake where water is collected and stored.

sediment: sand, mud, or gravel carried by a river.

sinkhole: a pit made when ground collapses after water breaks down rock under the surface.

species: types of animals or plants that are alike in many ways.

volcano: a mountain that builds up by eruptions of red-hot liquid rock from under Earth's surface.

More Books to Read

The Amazing Water Book
Deborah Seed
(Kids Can Press)

Rivers, Lakes, and Ponds
Eric Braun and Sandra Donovan
(Raintree, Steck-Vaughn)

Disappearing Lake
Debbie Miller
(Walker)

What's Inside Lakes?
Jane Kelly Kosek
(Powerkids Press)

 # Web Sites

Freshwater Ecosystems
mbgnet.mobot.org/fresh/
index.htm

Living Lakes
www.livinglakes.org

Large Lakes
www.infoplease.com/ipa/
A0001777.html

T.E.A.C.H. Great Lakes
www.great-lakes.net/teach/

To find additional web sites, use a reliable search engine to find one or more of the following keywords: **fish, lake ecosystem, world lakes.**

 # Index